SEED TIME

IS A 90 DAY DEVOTIONAL THAT HELPS ONE TAKE TIME, TO PLANT THE WORD OF GOD IN THEIR LIFE. LUKE 8:11, DECLARES, THE SEED IS THE WORD OF GOD. THIS BOOK IS FULL OF GOD'S PROMISES, THAT WILL UNLOCK THE UNMEASURABLE POWER OF GOD, IN ONE'S LIFE!

BYRON L. ALDRIDGE

SEED TIME

A 90 DAY DEVOTIONAL THAT HELPS ONE TAKE TIME TO
PLANT THE WORD OF GOD IN THEIR LIFE

BYRON L. ALDRIDGE

THE SHIELD PUBLISHING

Copyright © 2020 by Byron L. Aldridge

Publishing Assistance provided by:
Michelle Morrow www.chellreads.com

The Bible. Authorized King James Version, Oxford UP, 1998.

This book is dedicated to our Lord and Savior Jesus Christ, my beautiful wife Patrice Aldridge, and two wonderful children Euri and Bre'onna Aldridge

Acknowledgments

Special thanks to the Shield of Faith Empowerment Center and partners, my parents Charles and Maxcine Aldridge, for birthing me into this world and raising me. My siblings, Angela, Austin, and Charles. My other parents Larry and Gwendolyn Gilliom and sister Tiffany.

Special thanks, to all of my family, and friends, that have supported me and prayed for me throughout ministry. Thanks to my pastors, Pastor Lovell Howard and Dr. Sharon Nesbitt, for their teaching and nurturing in ministry.

This book is to inspire those who enjoy the word of God. This book was birthed from daily affirmations and confessions, that has become evidence in Pastor Byron L. Aldridge's daily life. This book will help bring the word of God and faith alive in one's life!

Pastor Byron L. Aldridge has overcome many challenges in life. He is sharing secrets, to becoming better, for those who struggle with doubt, failure, let downs, and unbelief.

SEED TIME, is a 90 day devotional that helps one, take time, to plant the word of God in their life. Luke 8:11, declares The seed is the word of God. This book is full of God's promises, that will unlock the immeasurable power of God, in one's life!

Prayer For The Reader

This book is published to increase your faith by declaring the word of God with daily affirmations and confessions. As you begin to confess and affirm the word of God, the Holy Spirit will begin to speak to you! Schedule and make time to meditate on the word of God and journal in the pages provided, to help you become closer with God. Meditating while journaling will cause your faith to increase and provide a clearer understanding of what you are affirming and confessing. If necessary, take time to search the scriptures, to provide more understanding. If possible, read the affirmations and confessions out loud, because according to Romans 10:17, faith come by hearing and hearing by the word of God.

God's will for each believer is they prosper in every area of their lives. Jesus declares in John 10:10, that he came that we may have life and life more abundantly. God's intention for humankind is their lives are enhanced by his finished work on the cross! I'm excited what is going to take place as you affirm and confess the word of God over your life. I pray as you read this book and journal, the Holy Spirit will enlighten your eyes and you may know what the hope of your calling is, in Christ Jesus. I pray you prosper and be in health, even as your soul prospers and your total man is strengthened spirit, soul, and body. I pray that restoration will take place in your life and you will remain in the faith!

I pray as you confess and affirm the word of God, your faith is increased, and you are strengthened by God's might and power. I pray the supernatural power of God would be released in your life and you prosper in all that you set your mind to do. I pray God will grant you supernatural increase and cause you to exceed in all your endeavors and prosper everything your hands touch. I pray God will grant you supernatural favor and doors are opened concerning your destiny and purpose. I pray grace and peace is multiplied to you and God reveal his perfect will for your life.

I pray that you are confident in your walk with God and all barriers, bondage, borders, and boundaries are removed from your life. I pray that you will trust God's divine timing and you will receive God's unmerited favor and mercy in your life. I pray you will be steadfast and unmovable always abounding in the work of Lord. I pray you are consistent in your faith and will not allow fear and the cares of the world choke out the word of God. I pray you receive the word of God and your heart is good ground which bring forth and bear more and much fruit.

Lastly, I pray your faith, family, and finances are increased!

Father I thank YOU that YOU hear me and hear me always, I thank YOU for clean hands and a pure heart. I thank YOU for cleansing me from all unrighteousness and renewing the right spirit within me.

John 11:41-42, Psalm 24:3-4, Psalm 51:10

Daily Confessions and Affirmations

I come boldly to the throne of grace that I may obtain mercy and find grace to help me in my time of need.

Hebrews 4:16

Daily Confessions and Affirmations

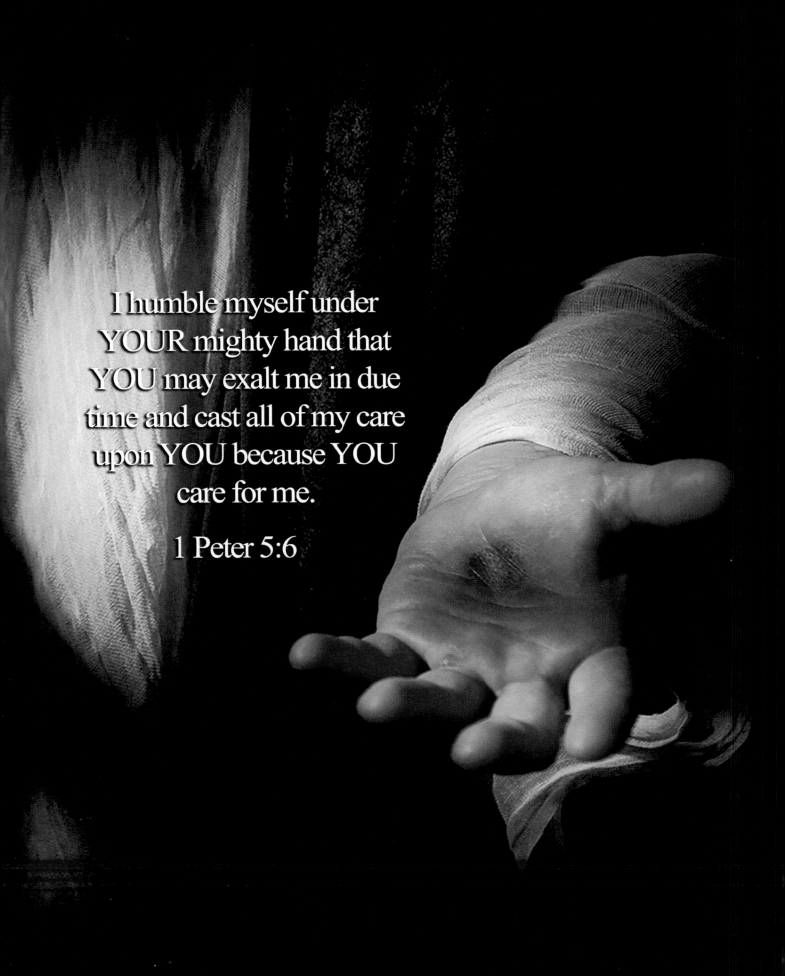

I humble myself under YOUR mighty hand that YOU may exalt me in due time and cast all of my care upon YOU because YOU care for me.

1 Peter 5:6

Daily Confessions and Affirmations

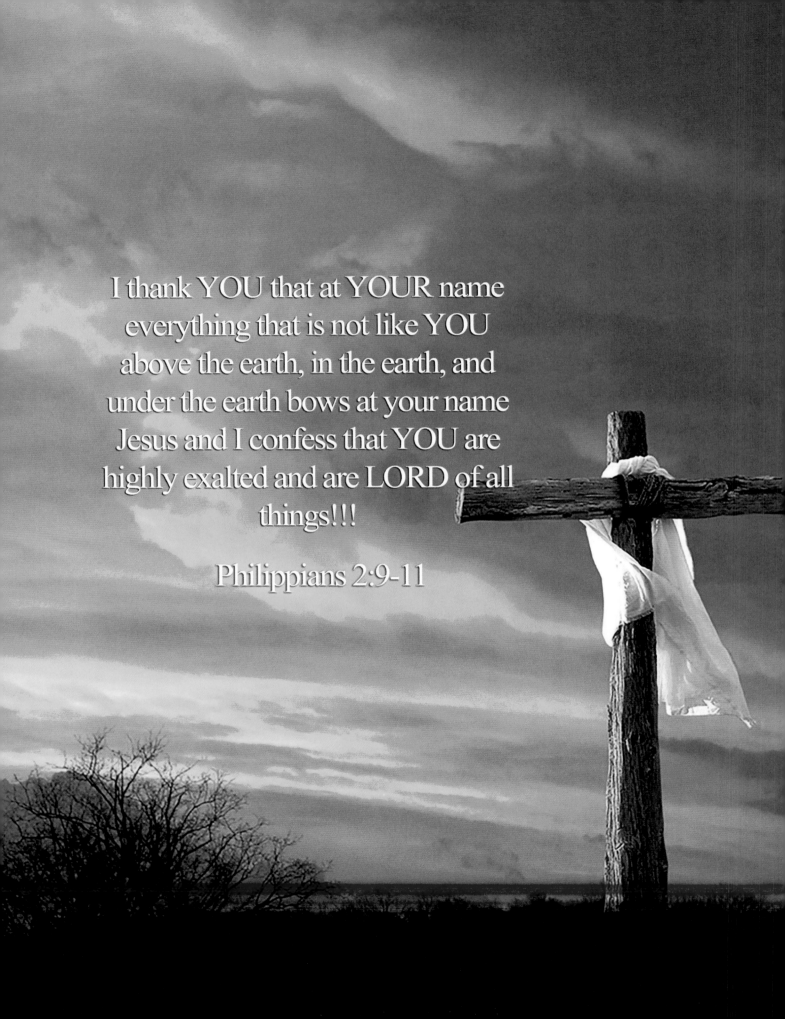

I thank YOU that at YOUR name
everything that is not like YOU
above the earth, in the earth, and
under the earth bows at your name
Jesus and I confess that YOU are
highly exalted and are LORD of all
things!!!

Philippians 2:9-11

Daily Confessions and Affirmations

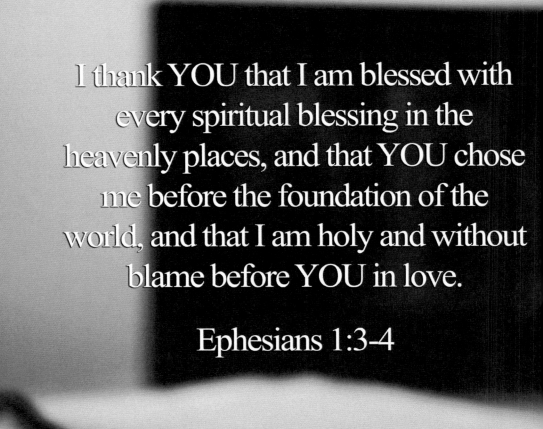

I thank YOU that I am blessed with every spiritual blessing in the heavenly places, and that YOU chose me before the foundation of the world, and that I am holy and without blame before YOU in love.

Ephesians 1:3-4

Daily Confessions and Affirmations

_____

_____

_____

_____

_____

_____

_____

_____

_____

_____

_____

_____

_____

_____

_____

_____

_____

Plant the Word of God in to Your Life

I thank YOU Father of glory, that YOU have given me the spirit of wisdom and revelation in the knowledge of YOU, and that the eyes of my understanding are enlightened, and that I know the hope of YOUR calling, what the riches of YOUR glory of YOUR inheritance in us the saints, and what YOUR exceeding greatness of YOUR power in us who believe according to the working of YOUR mighty power.

Ephesians 1:17-19

Daily Confessions and Affirmations

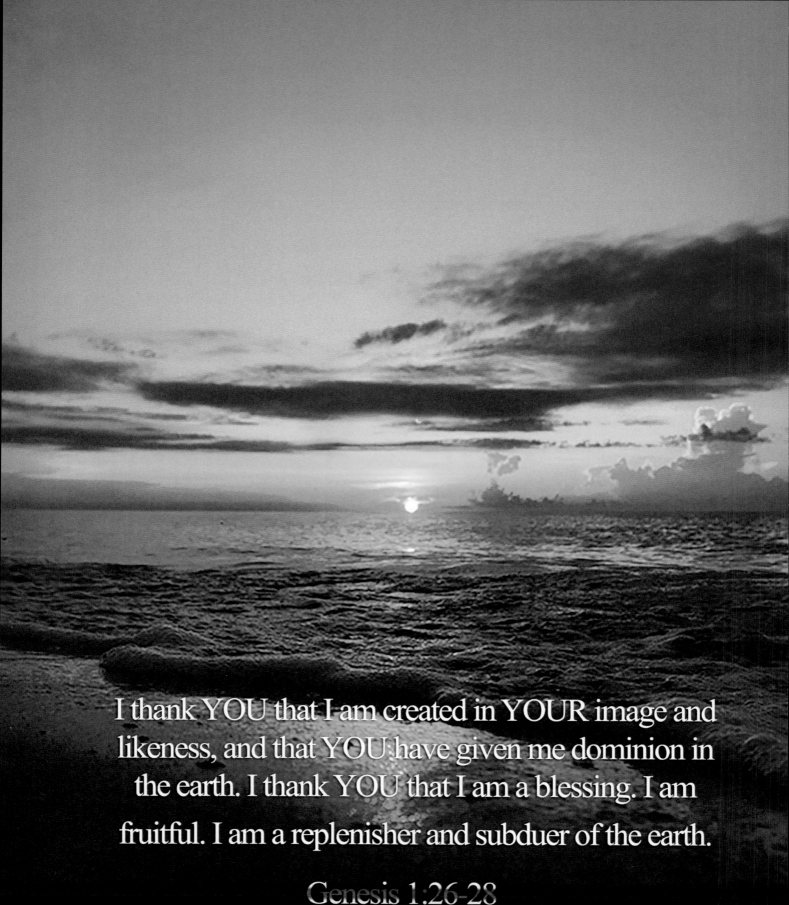

I thank YOU that I am created in YOUR image and likeness, and that YOU have given me dominion in the earth. I thank YOU that I am a blessing. I am fruitful. I am a replenisher and subduer of the earth.

Genesis 1:26-28

Daily Confessions and Affirmations

_____

_____

_____

_____

_____

_____

_____

_____

_____

_____

_____

_____

_____

_____

_____

_____

_____

_____

I thank YOU that I am justified by faith, and have peace with YOU through our LORD Jesus Christ that I now have access by faith into this grace wherein I stand, and rejoice in hope of the glory of God. I glory in tribulations, knowing that tribulation, work patience, and patience, experience, and experience hope; and hope make me not ashamed, because YOUR love is shed abroad in my heart by the Holy Ghost which is given for me.

Romans 5:1-5

Daily Confessions and Affirmations

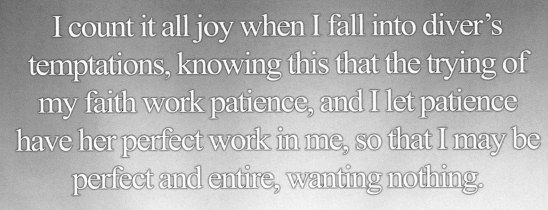

I count it all joy when I fall into diver's temptations, knowing this that the trying of my faith work patience, and I let patience have her perfect work in me, so that I may be perfect and entire, wanting nothing.

James 1:2-3

Daily Confessions and Affirmations

I thank you that all things work together for my good because I love YOU, and am the called according to YOUR purpose. I thank YOU that YOU called, justified, and glorified me. I thank YOU for the things that were meant for evil, and YOU turn it for my good.

Romans 8:28-29, Genesis 50: 20

Daily Confessions and Affirmations

_____

_____

_____

_____

_____

_____

_____

_____

_____

_____

_____

_____

_____

_____

_____

_____

_____

Plant the Word of God in to Your Life

I thank YOU for YOUR great love with which I am saved, even when I was dead in trespasses and sin, YOU made me alive together with Christ and (by grace I am saved) and raised us up together, and made me sit together in the heavenly places in Christ Jesus.

Ephesians 2:4-6

Daily Confessions and Affirmations

I thank YOU that I am a new creation, old things have
passed away, and all things have become new.

2 Corinthians 5:17

Daily Confessions and Affirmations

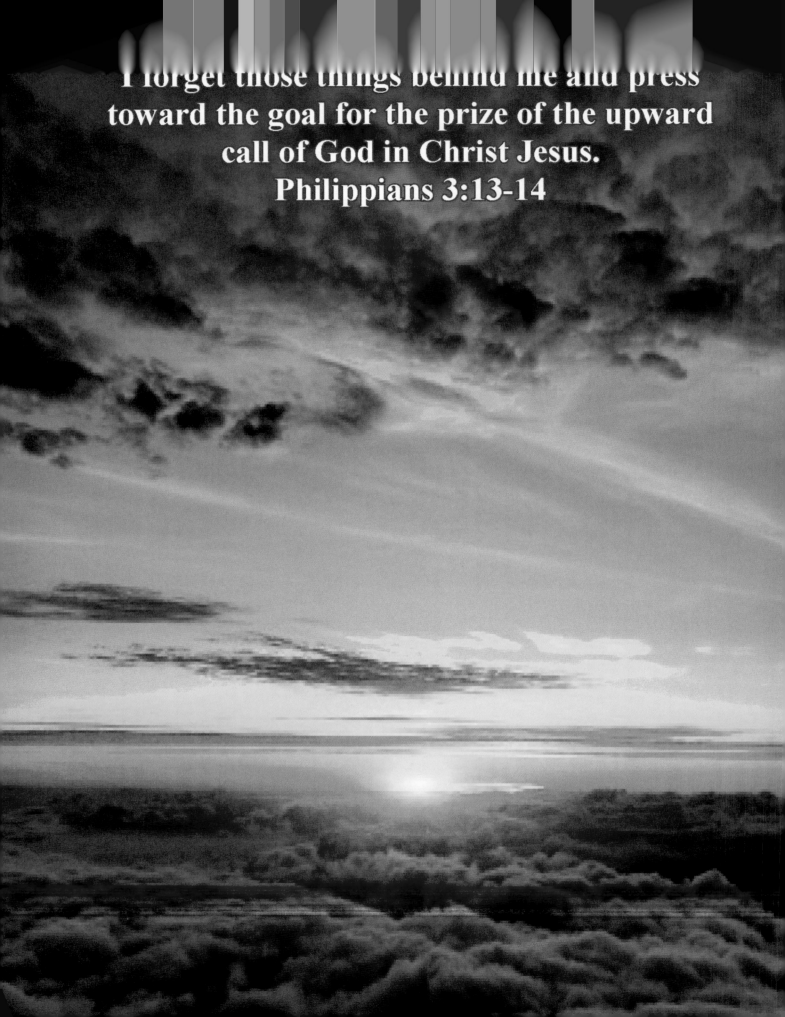

I forget those things behind me and press toward the goal for the prize of the upward call of God in Christ Jesus.
Philippians 3:13-14

Daily Confessions and Affirmations

I do not remember the former things nor
consider the things of old because of the
new things that YOU are doing in my life.

Isaiah 43:18-19

Daily Confessions and Affirmations

I am increasing in wisdom, statue, and in favor
with YOU and men.

Luke 2:52, 1 Samuel 2:26

Daily Confessions and Affirmations

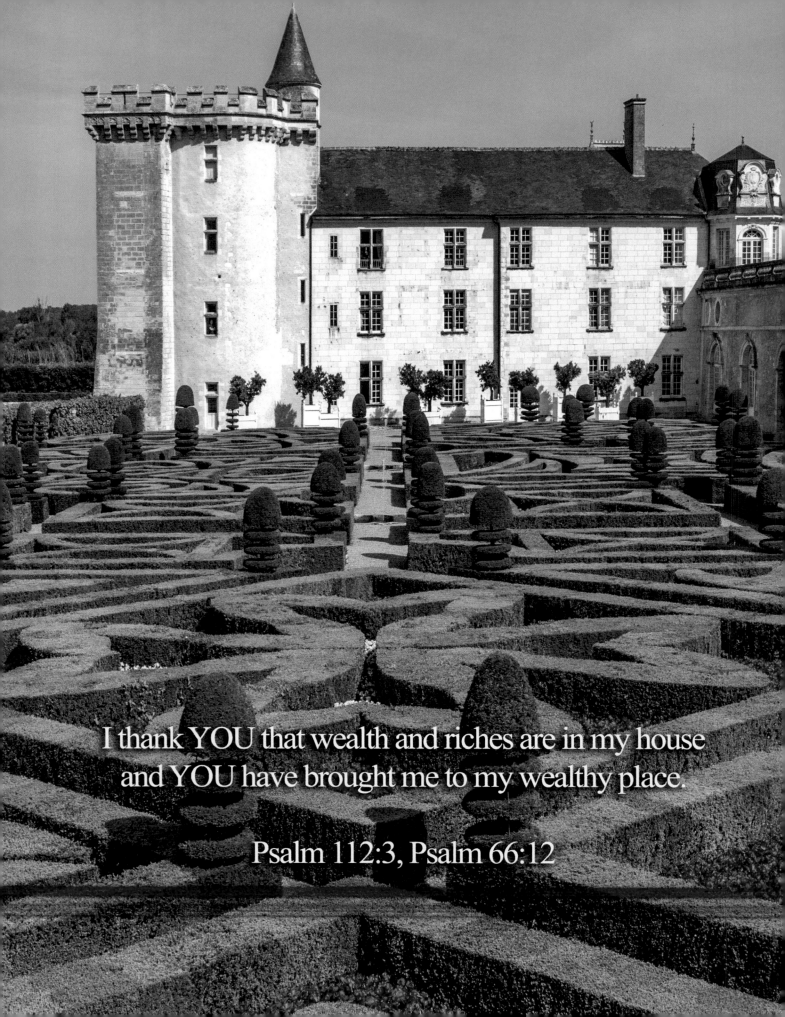

I thank YOU that wealth and riches are in my house
and YOU have brought me to my wealthy place.

Psalm 112:3, Psalm 66:12

Daily Confessions and Affirmations

_____

_____

_____

_____

_____

_____

_____

_____

_____

_____

_____

_____

_____

_____

_____

_____

Plant the Word of God in to Your Life

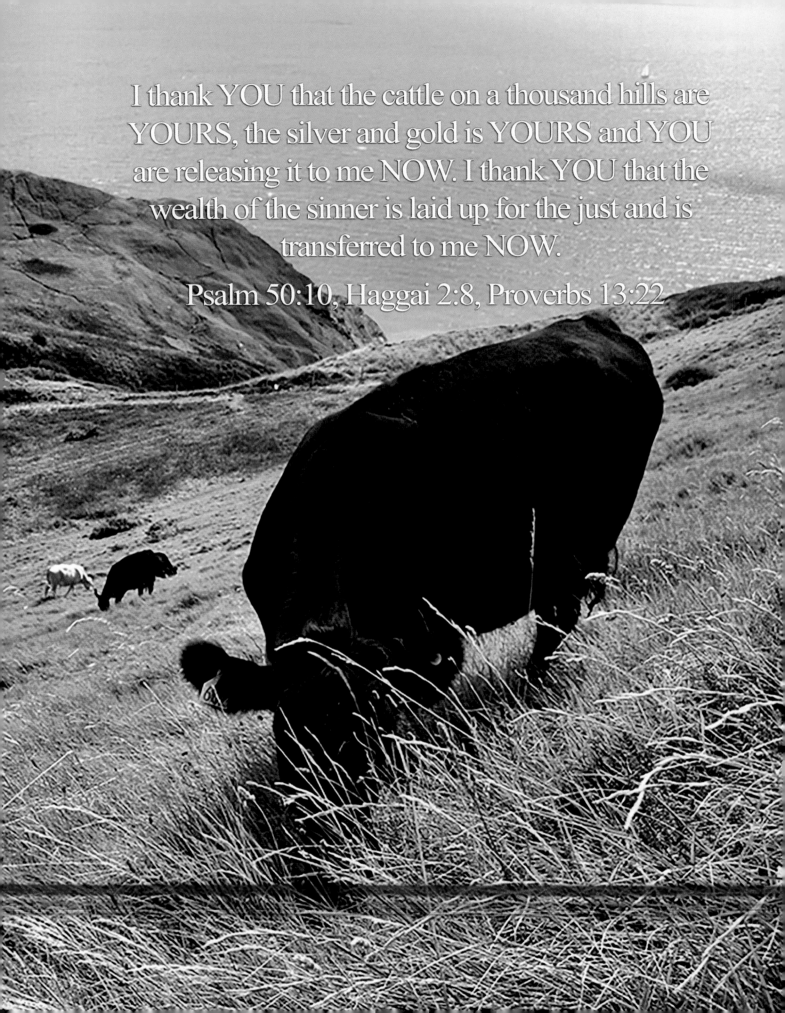

I thank YOU that the cattle on a thousand hills are YOURS, the silver and gold is YOURS and YOU are releasing it to me NOW. I thank YOU that the wealth of the sinner is laid up for the just and is transferred to me NOW.

Psalm 50:10, Haggai 2:8, Proverbs 13:22

Daily Confessions and Affirmations

I thank you for it is God that gives me power to get wealth, that He may establish His covenant which He sware unto my fathers, Abraham, Isaac, and Jacob.

Deuteronomy 8:18

Daily Confessions and Affirmations

I bless YOU LORD, with my soul and forget not all YOUR benefits and I thank YOU that I am daily loaded with benefits.

Psalm 103:2, Psalm 68:19

Daily Confessions and Affirmations

I am blessed in the city, blessed in field. I am blessed in the fruit of my body, the fruit of my ground. Blessed is my basket and store, I am blessed going out and blessed coming in. The LORD shall command the blessing upon me in the storehouses, and everything I set my hands to and the land, which the LORD gives me. The LORD shall establish me a holy people unto himself. All of the people of the earth shall see that I am called by the name of the LORD, and they shall be afraid of me. The LORD shall make me plenteous in goods, in the fruit of my body, and the fruit of my cattle, and in the fruit of my ground. The LORD shall open unto me his good treasures of heaven to give me rain unto my land in it season and to bless all the work of my hands and I shall lend unto many nations and not borrow. I am the head and not the tail, and I am above only, and I shall not be beneath.

Deuteronomy 28: 2-13

Daily Confessions and Affirmations

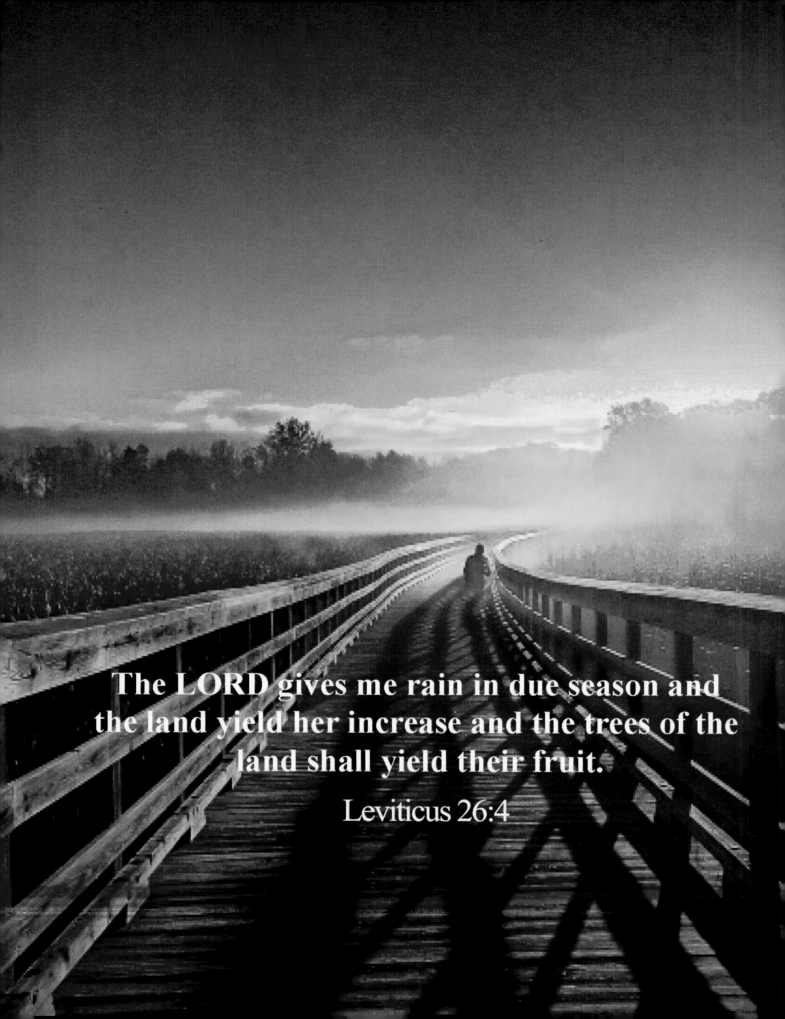

The LORD gives me rain in due season and the land yield her increase and the trees of the land shall yield their fruit.

Leviticus 26:4

Daily Confessions and Affirmations

_____
_____
_____
_____
_____
_____
_____
_____
_____
_____
_____
_____
_____
_____
_____
_____
_____

Plant the Word of God in to Your Life

I love the LORD and He blesses me, multiplies me, and blesses the fruit of my womb, fruit of my land, my corn, wine, and my oil, the increase of my kine, and the flocks of my sheep, in the land which he swore unto the fathers to give me. My bank accounts are full, plenteous, and overflowing. The LORD takes away all sickness and evil diseases.

Deuteronomy 7:13, 15

Daily Confessions and Affirmations

_____

_____

_____

_____

_____

_____

_____

_____

_____

_____

_____

_____

_____

_____

_____

_____

_____

_____

My beginning was small, but my latter end
shall greatly increase.

Job 8:7

Daily Confessions and Affirmations

The LORD increases my greatness and comforts me on every side.

Psalm 71:21

Daily Confessions and Affirmations

The LORD shall give unto me that which is good and
my land shall yield her increase
Psalm 85:12

Daily Confessions and Affirmations

The LORD increases me more
and more, me and my children.

Psalm 115:14

Daily Confessions and Affirmations

_____

_____

_____

_____

_____

_____

_____

_____

_____

_____

_____

_____

_____

_____

_____

_____

I decrease, so that Jesus and the
Holy Spirit increase in my life.

John 3:30

Daily Confessions and Affirmations

The LORD blesses those who blesses me, and
curses those who curse me.

Genesis 12:3

Daily Confessions and Affirmations

The LORD has given me dominion over the works of
thy hands, and has put all things under my feet.

Psalm 8:6

Daily Confessions and Affirmations

_____

_____

_____

_____

_____

_____

_____

_____

_____

_____

_____

_____

_____

_____

_____

The LORD is my shepherd and I have no wants. He restores my soul and leads me in the paths of righteousness for His name's sake. He prepares a table for me in the presence of my enemies, He anoints my head with oil and my cup runs over. Goodness and mercy follow me all the days of my life.

Psalm 23

Daily Confessions and Affirmations

I thank YOU for beginning a good work in me and performing it until the day of Jesus Christ. I thank YOU for being the author and finisher of my faith.

Philippians 1:6, Hebrews 12:2

Daily Confessions and Affirmations

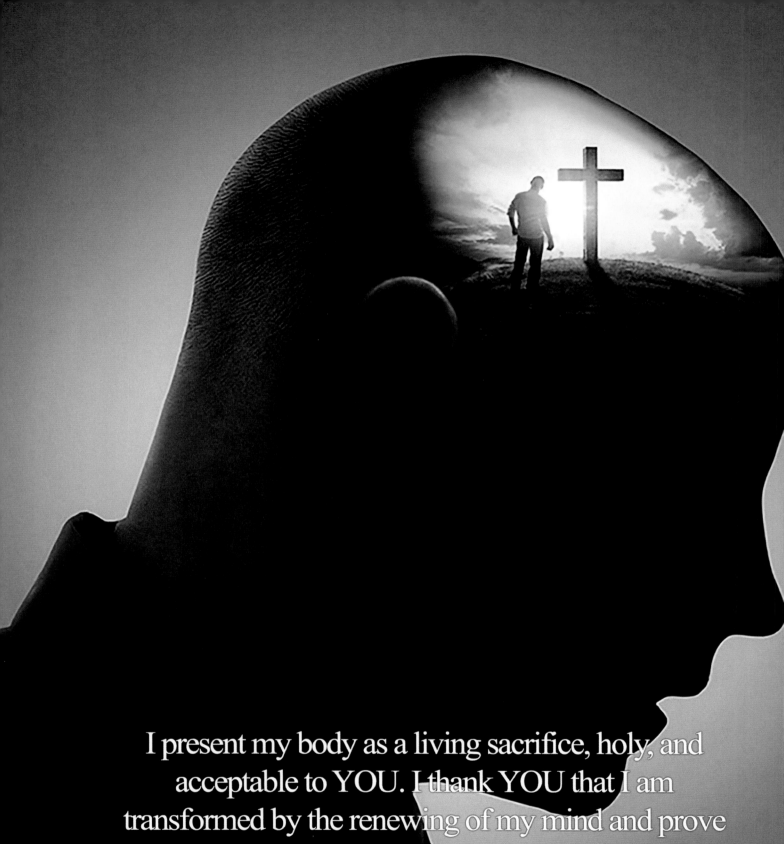

I present my body as a living sacrifice, holy, and acceptable to YOU. I thank YOU that I am transformed by the renewing of my mind and prove what the good, acceptable, and perfect will of God is concerning my life.
Romans 12:1-2

Daily Confessions and Affirmations

Plant the Word of God in to Your Life

I will praise the LORD for I am fearfully and wonderfully made.

Psalm 139:14

Daily Confessions and Affirmations

I thank you that me and my spouse walk together and are in agreement, we thank you that whatever we bind on earth shall be bound in heaven: and whatever we loose on earth shall be loosed in heaven. We thank you whatever we agree on earth as touching anything that we shall ask, it will be done for us of our Father which is in heaven.
Amos 3:3, Matthew 18:18-19

Daily Confessions and Affirmations

Plant the Word of God in to Your Life

I thank YOU for supernatural debt cancellations and ratifications. I decree and declare that I walk in divine prosperity and divine purpose of God. I send YOUR word forth to accomplish every promise in Jesus name. I thank YOU that YOUR word is making things bud and that it accomplishes everything YOU sent it to do.

Isaiah 55:1-13, 2 Kings 4:1-7

Daily Confessions and Affirmations

_____

_____

_____

_____

_____

_____

_____

_____

_____

_____

_____

_____

_____

_____

_____

_____

_____

_____

I thank YOU that I am YOUR anointed and YOU hold my right hand and open before me double doors, so that the gates will not be shut. I thank YOU that YOU go before me and make the crooked places straight and break in pieces the gates of bronze and cut the bars of iron. I thank YOU for the treasures of darkness and hidden riches of secret places.

Isaiah 45:1-3

Daily Confessions and Affirmations

I thank YOU that YOU have commanded others to bless me SUPERNATURALLY and have commanded others to SUPERNATURALLY pay debts for me!!
1Kings 17:1-14, 2Kings 4:1-7

Daily Confessions and Affirmations

_____

_____

_____

_____

_____

_____

_____

_____

_____

_____

_____

_____

_____

_____

_____

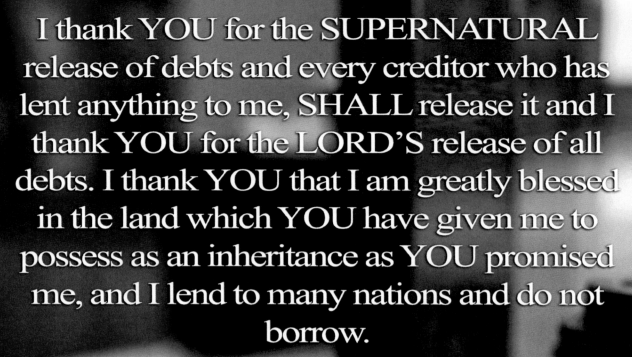

I thank YOU for the SUPERNATURAL release of debts and every creditor who has lent anything to me, SHALL release it and I thank YOU for the LORD'S release of all debts. I thank YOU that I am greatly blessed in the land which YOU have given me to possess as an inheritance as YOU promised me, and I lend to many nations and do not borrow.
Deuteronomy15:1-6

Daily Confessions and Affirmations

I thank you for my marriage, two is better than one, and we have a good reward of our labor. If one fall, the other will lift the other up. Ecclesiastes 4:9-10

Daily Confessions and Affirmations

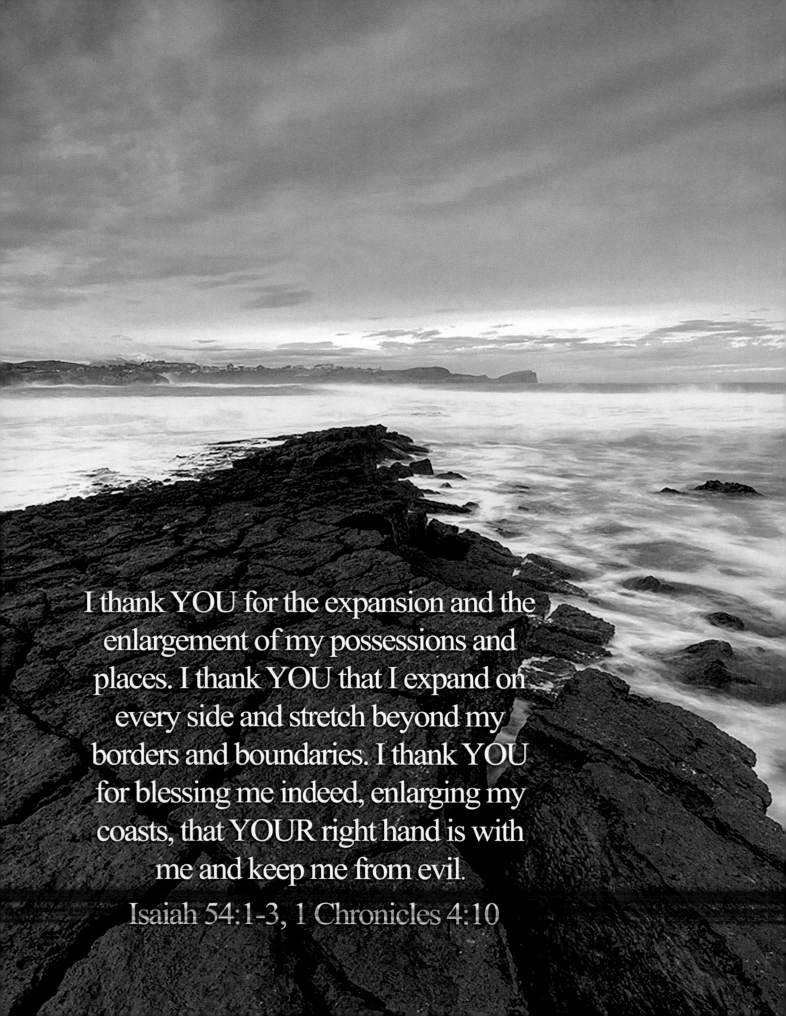

I thank YOU for the expansion and the enlargement of my possessions and places. I thank YOU that I expand on every side and stretch beyond my borders and boundaries. I thank YOU for blessing me indeed, enlarging my coasts, that YOUR right hand is with me and keep me from evil.

Isaiah 54:1-3, 1 Chronicles 4:10

Daily Confessions and Affirmations

_____

_____

_____

_____

_____

_____

_____

_____

_____

_____

_____

_____

_____

_____

_____

_____

I am filled with the spirit of God, in wisdom, understanding, knowledge, and in all manner of workmanship.

Exodus 31:3

Daily Confessions and Affirmations

My heart speaks wisdom and the meditations of my
heart shall be of understanding.
Psalm 49:3

Daily Confessions and Affirmations

The spirit of the LORD rests upon me, the
spirit of wisdom and understanding, the spirit
of counsel and might, the spirit of knowledge
and the fear of the Lord.

Isaiah 11:2

Daily Confessions and Affirmations

I thank YOU for breaking generational curses off my life, children, grandchildren, siblings, and bloodline in Jesus Name! Thank YOU for forgiving me and my forefathers and clearing the guilt and iniquities of us all.

Exodus 34:7, Numbers 14:18

Daily Confessions and Affirmations

I thank YOU that YOU were wounded for my transgressions and bruised for my iniquities and the chastisenment of my peace is on YOU. I walk in divine healing and every disease, germ, bacteria, virus, unclean thing that touches my body dies instantly in the name of Jesus, and with YOUR stripes I am healed.
Isaiah 53:5

Daily Confessions and Affirmations

I thank YOU for baring my sins in YOUR body on the tree and taking the curse for me. I thank YOU for blotting out the ordinances that were against me, which were contrary to me, by taking it out the way, and nailing it to the cross.

1 Peter 2:24, Galatians 3:13, Colossians 1:20

Daily Confessions and Affirmations

Plant the Word of God in to Your Life

I THANK YOU that you forgive me of all my iniquities, and heal me of all and every sickness and disease.

Psalm 103:3

Daily Confessions and Affirmations

I thank YOU that YOU heal the broken in heart, and bind up their wounds.

Psalm 34:1-3

Daily Confessions and Affirmations

I thank YOU that it is of YOUR mercies that I am not consumed, because YOUR compassions fail not, they are new every morning: great is thy faithfulness. YOU are my portion, saith my soul therefore I will hope in YOU

Lamentations 3:22-24

Daily Confessions and Affirmations

Plant the Word of God in to Your Life

I will bless YOU LORD at all times and YOUR praise, shall continually be in my mouth. My soul makes a boast in YOU LORD, and I magnify and exalt YOUR name.

Psalm 34:1-3

Daily Confessions and Affirmations

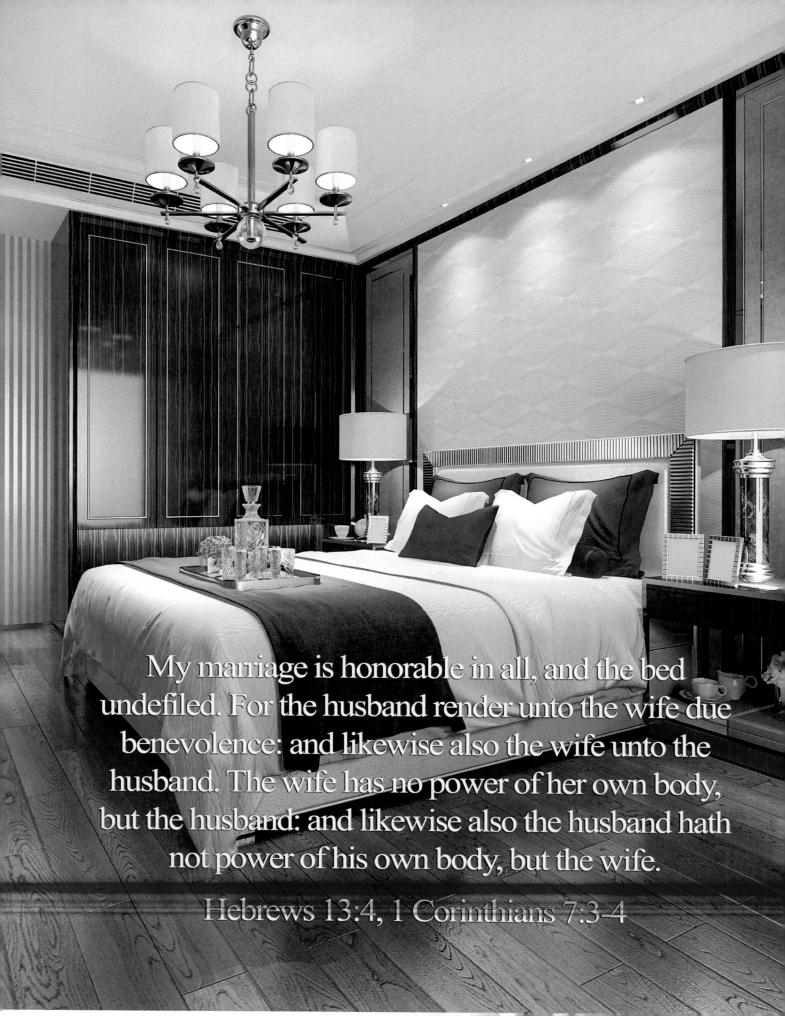

My marriage is honorable in all, and the bed undefiled. For the husband render unto the wife due benevolence: and likewise also the wife unto the husband. The wife has no power of her own body, but the husband: and likewise also the husband hath not power of his own body, but the wife.

Hebrews 13:4, 1 Corinthians 7:3-4

Daily Confessions and Affirmations

I thank YOU that YOU restore health unto me, and heal me of every wound emotionally, physically, socially, and spiritually.
Jeremiah 30:17

Daily Confessions and Affirmations

I thank YOU that YOU restore the years that the locust, cankerworm, caterpillar, and palmerworm have eaten. I eat in plenty and am satisfied, and I give praise to YOUR name. I thank YOU that my floors are full of wheat, vats overflowing with new wine and oil and I will never be ashamed. I thank YOU for pouring out YOUR Spirit on all flesh, YOUR sons and daughters prophesy, old men dream dreams, and young men see visions.

Joel 2:24-29

Daily Confessions and Affirmations

I thank YOU that I am strengthened with might by YOUR SPIRIT in my inner man . I thank YOU that I do exceedingly and abundantly above all, I ask or think according to YOUR power working inside me!

Ephesians 3:16, 20

Daily Confessions and Affirmations

The LORD teaches me how to profit and leads me the way I should go.

Isaiah 48:17

Daily Confessions and Affirmations

The LORD has called me from the womb, from the bowels of my mother hath he made mention of my name. The LORD has made my mouth like a sharp sword; in the shadow of his hand hath he hid me, and made me a polished shaft; in his quiver hath he hid me.

Isaiah 49:1-2

Daily Confessions and Affirmations

The LORD has given me the tongue of the
learned, that I should know how to speak a
word in season, to him that is weary, he
wakens me morning by morning, and he
wakens my ears to hear as the learned.

Isaiah 50:4

Daily Confessions and Affirmations

I thank YOU that YOUR ways are not my ways, and YOUR thoughts are not my thoughts, but they are higher than mine. I trust YOUR divine calendar, plan, timeline, and timetable on my behalf.

Isaiah 55:8-9

Daily Confessions and Affirmations

Plant the Word of God in to Your Life

No weapon that is formed against me shall prosper; and every tongue that shall rise against me in judgment I condemn. I come against every ill spoken word, curse, witchcraft prayer, warlock prayer, negative word, demonic, satanic and luciferin spirit in the name of Jesus, and return it back double fold. I apply the blood of Jesus over every negative and idle word in Jesus name.

Isaiah 54:17

Daily Confessions and Affirmations

_____

_____

_____

_____

_____

_____

_____

_____

_____

_____

_____

_____

_____

_____

_____

_____

CUTOFF

The spirit of the LORD is upon me, because the LORD has anointed me to preach good tidings to the meek, he has sent me to bind up the brokenhearted, to proclaim liberty to the captives, and the opening of the prison to them that are bound. I thank YOU that you have given me beauty for ashes, the oil of joy for mourning, the garment of praise for the spirit of heaviness, the planting of the LORD, that YOU may be glorified.

Isaiah 61:1-3

Daily Confessions and Affirmations

_____

_____

_____

_____

_____

_____

_____

_____

_____

_____

_____

_____

_____

_____

_____

I put my trust in YOU and I will not be ashamed, and my enemies shall not triumph over me.

Psalm 25:2

Daily Confessions and Affirmations

I thank YOU God, because YOU always cause me to triumph in Christ, and make manifest the savor of YOUR knowledge by me in every place.

2 Corinthians 2:14

Daily Confessions and Affirmations

Plant the Word of God in to Your Life

I thank YOU that nothing shall separate me from YOUR love, and I am more than a conqueror through YOU because YOU love me.

Romans 8:35-39

Daily Confessions and Affirmations

I thank YOU for thoughts of peace towards me, and not of evil, to give me an expected end.

Jeremiah 29:11

Daily Confessions and Affirmations

Wealth and riches finds me and they are in my house
and I thank YOU for money that it answers all things.

Psalm 112:3, Ecclesiastes 10:19

Daily Confessions and Affirmations

Plant the Word of God in to Your Life

I walk in the Spirit, so I do not fulfill the lust of the flesh. I thank YOU for the fruit of the Spirit which is love, joy, peace, longsuffering, gentleness, goodness, faith, meekness, and temperance.

Galatians 5:16, 22-23

Daily Confessions and Affirmations

I thank YOU that the weapons of my warfare are not carnal, but mighty through YOU to the pulling down of strong holds, casting down imaginations, and every high thing that exalts itself against the knowledge of YOU and I bring into captivity every thought to the obedience of Christ in Jesus Name!!!

2 Corinthians 10:4-5

Daily Confessions and Affirmations

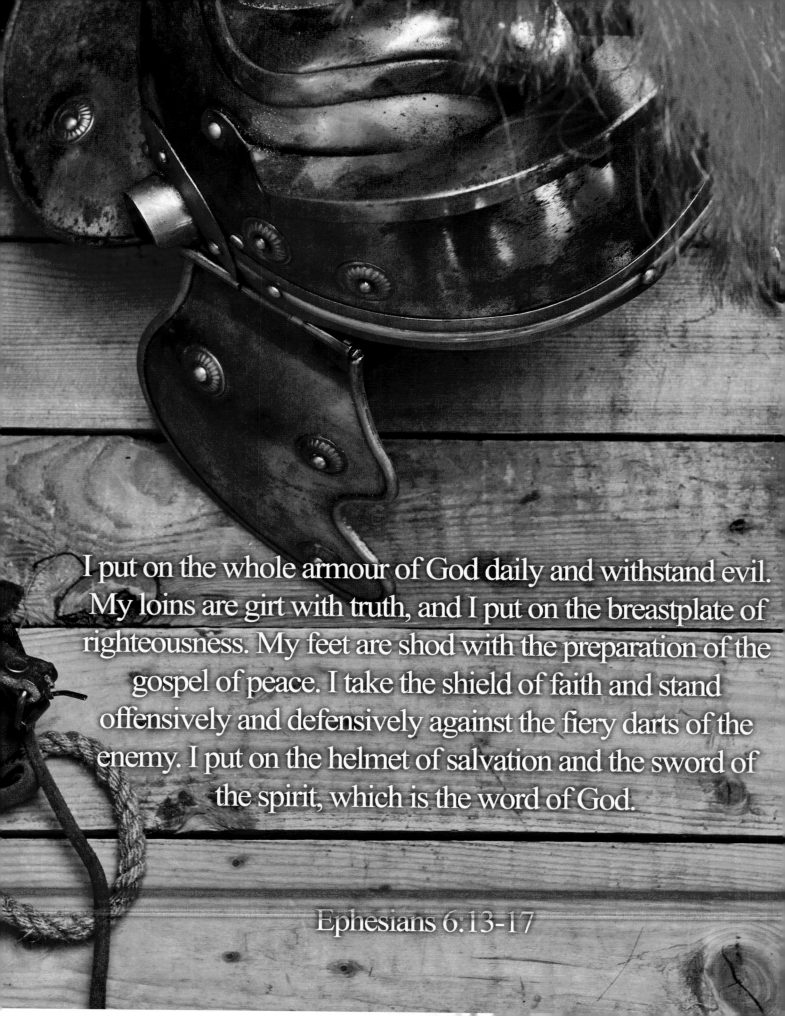

I put on the whole armour of God daily and withstand evil. My loins are girt with truth, and I put on the breastplate of righteousness. My feet are shod with the preparation of the gospel of peace. I take the shield of faith and stand offensively and defensively against the fiery darts of the enemy. I put on the helmet of salvation and the sword of the spirit, which is the word of God.

Ephesians 6.13-17

Daily Confessions and Affirmations

I thank YOU that YOUR Word is nigh me in my mouth and in my heart, the Word of faith. I decree and declare that every word and every promise come forth to me in Jesus name. I call nothing into something and something out of nothing to come forth into full manifestation according to the word of God and that it is established in Jesus name. I call those things that are not as though they were. I am a King and issue the decree now that it comes to pass quickly, swiftly, and expediently in Jesus name!!

Romans 10:8, Job 22:28, Romans 4:17

Daily Confessions and Affirmations

Plant the Word of God in to Your Life

Grace and peace is multiplied unto me through the knowledge of GOD, and of Jesus my LORD, according as HIS divine power hath given unto me all things that pertain unto life and godliness, through the knowledge of HIM, that hath called me to glory and virtue: whereby are given unto me exceeding great and precious promises: that by these I am a partakers of the divine nature, having escaped the corruption that is in the world through lust.

2 Peter 1:3-4

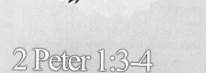

Daily Confessions and Affirmations

I submit myself one to another in the fear of God. The wife submits herself to the husband as unto the Lord. The Husband loves the wife as his own body and is joined unto the wife and the two are one flesh. I won't allow anyone or anything separate us for what God has joined together, let no man put asunder.

Ephesians 5:21-23; 28-31, Mark 5:32

Daily Confessions and Affirmations

Plant the Word of God in to Your Life

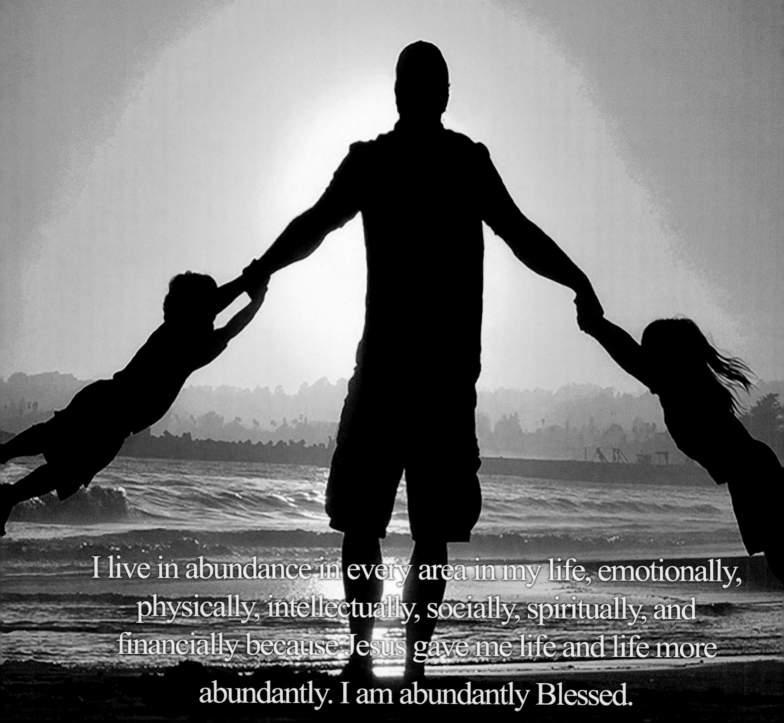

I live in abundance in every area in my life, emotionally, physically, intellectually, socially, spiritually, and financially because Jesus gave me life and life more abundantly. I am abundantly Blessed.

John 10:10

Daily Confessions and Affirmations

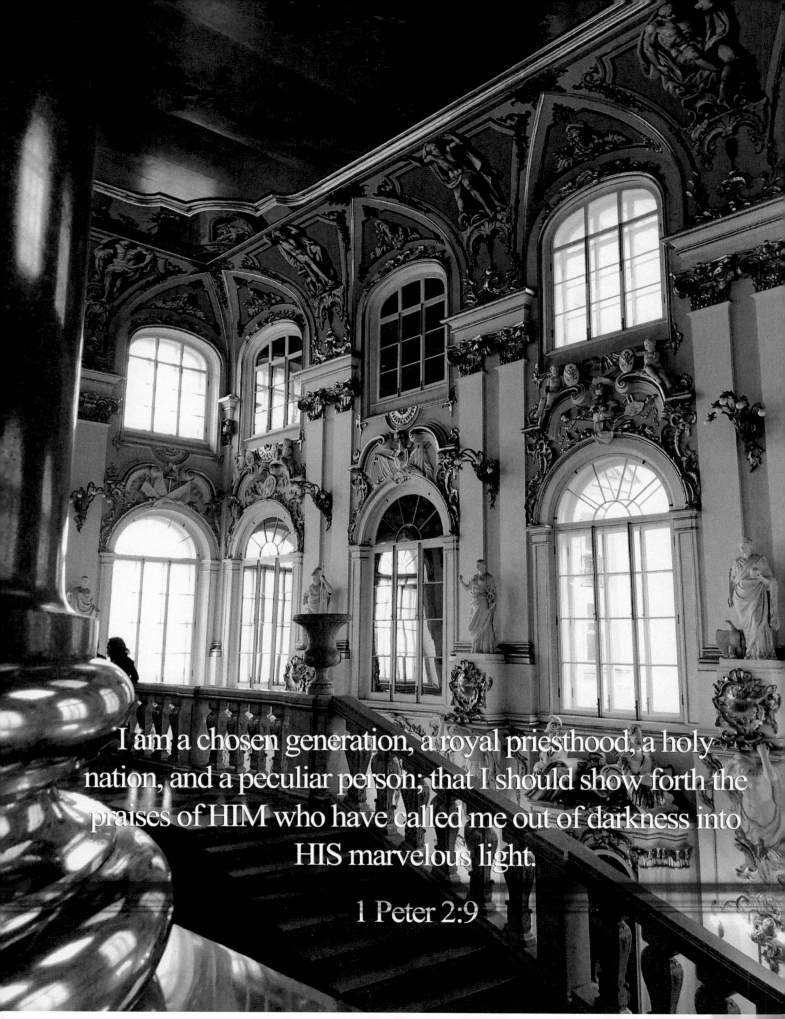

I am a chosen generation, a royal priesthood, a holy nation, and a peculiar person; that I should show forth the praises of HIM who have called me out of darkness into HIS marvelous light.

1 Peter 2:9

Daily Confessions and Affirmations

Plant the Word of God in to Your Life

Greater is HE that is in me than he that is in the world.

1 John 4:4

Daily Confessions and Affirmations

Plant the Word of God in to Your Life

I am a heir to God and joint heir to
Jesus Christ.

Romans 8:17

Daily Confessions and Affirmations

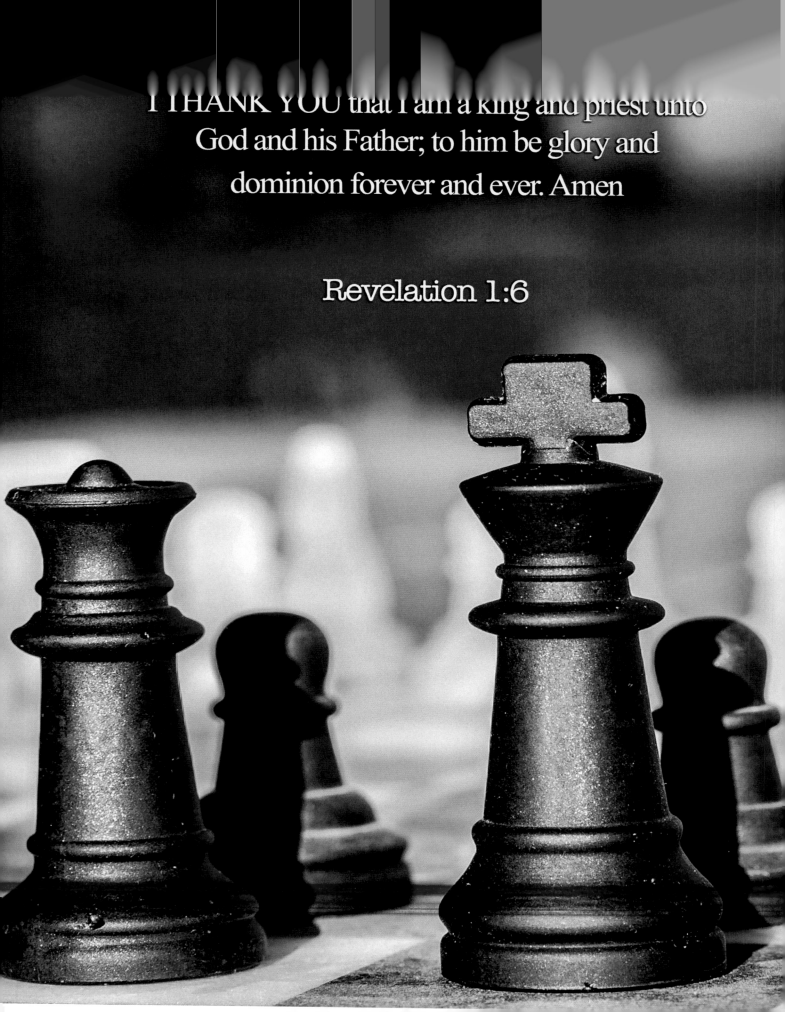

I THANK YOU that I am a king and priest unto God and his Father; to him be glory and dominion forever and ever. Amen

Revelation 1:6

Daily Confessions and Affirmations

Christ has redeemed me from the curse of the law, being made a curse for me: for it is written; Cursed is every one that hangs on a tree: that the blessing of Abraham might come on the Gentiles through Jesus Christ; that I might receive the promise of the spirit through faith.

Galatians 3:13-14

Daily Confessions and Affirmations

I thank YOU LORD for the blessing, for it makes one rich, and adds no sorrow with it.

Proverbs 10:22

Daily Confessions and Affirmations

Plant the Word of God in to Your Life

LORD I thank YOU that YOU are not a man that YOU should lie, and a not a man that YOU should repent. Have you not said, and shall you not do it? Or have YOU not spoken, and shall YOU not make it good? Behold, I have received and thank YOU for the commandment to bless, and YOU have blessed and YOU cannot reverse it.

Numbers 23:19-20

Daily Confessions and Affirmations

I thank you angels that you are ministering
spirits and that you are excelling in strength that
do my commandments hearkening unto the
voice of my words.
Hebrews 1:7, Psalm 103:20

Daily Confessions and Affirmations

The LORD has given me power to tread on serpents and scorpions, and over all the power of the enemy: and nothing shall by any means hurt me.
Luke 10:19

Daily Confessions and Affirmations

Daily Confessions and Affirmations

Plant the Word of God in to Your Life

I am the king or the little god in the earth
and I am a child of the most High.
Psalms 82:6, John 10:34-35

Daily Confessions and Affirmations

My GOD, El Elyon, Jehovah Jireh, El Shaddai, and Jehovah Chayil, supplies all of my need according to his riches in glory by Christ Jesus.

Philippians 4:19

Daily Confessions and Affirmations

Every place that the sole of my feet tread upon GOD has given me, and I meditate on the word day and night and my ways are prosperous and I have good success.

Joshua 1:3, Joshua 1:8

Daily Confessions and Affirmations

My children are at the top of their class and obey their parents, for this is first commandment with promise that they will live long.

Ephesians 6:1-3

Daily Confessions and Affirmations

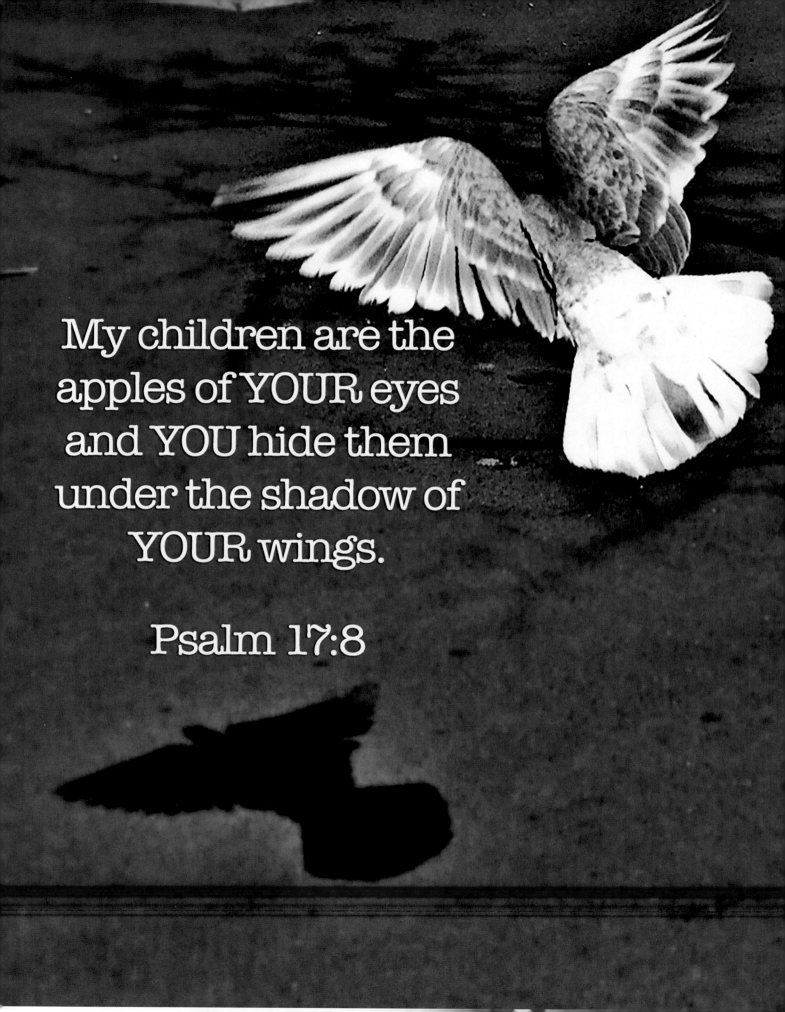

My children are the apples of YOUR eyes and YOU hide them under the shadow of YOUR wings.

Psalm 17:8

Daily Confessions and Affirmations

Plant the Word of God in to Your Life

I thank you that I have trained up my children, in the way they should go and as they grow older, they will not depart from it.

Proverbs 22:6

Daily Confessions and Affirmations

My children are taught of the LORD, and great shall be their peace.

Isaiah 54:13

Daily Confessions and Affirmations

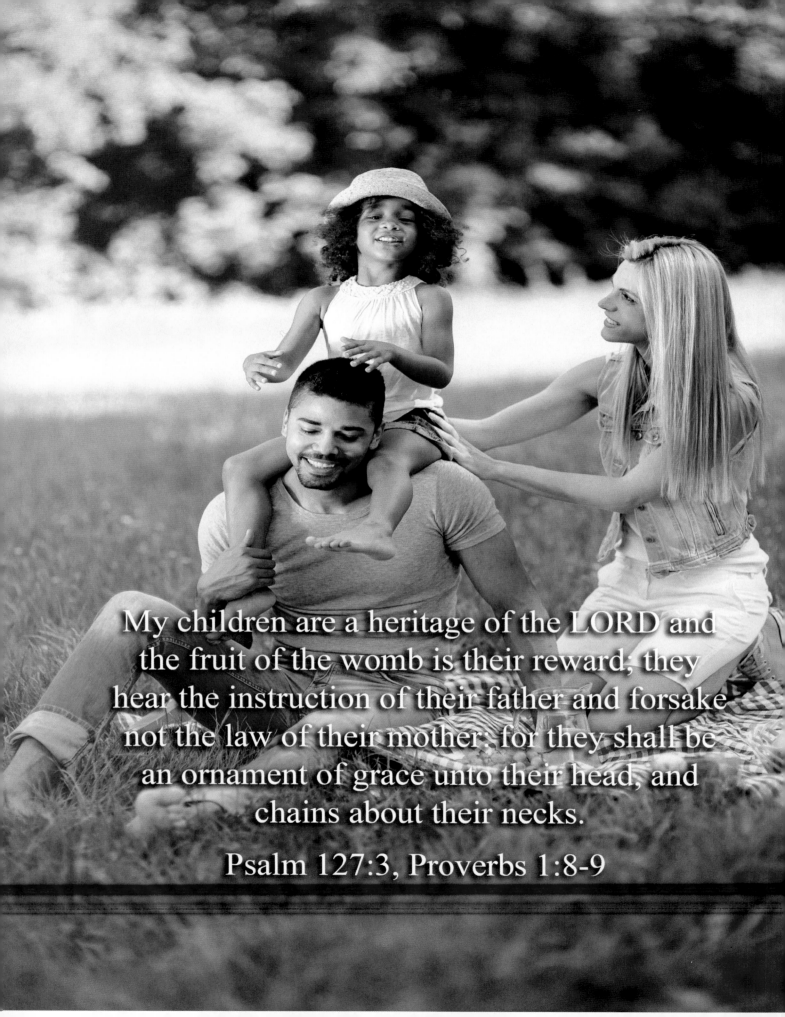

My children are a heritage of the LORD and the fruit of the womb is their reward; they hear the instruction of their father and forsake not the law of their mother; for they shall be an ornament of grace unto their head, and chains about their necks.

Psalm 127:3, Proverbs 1:8-9

Daily Confessions and Affirmations

Thank You...

I thank you for purchasing my 90 day devotional. I pray that you have found it to be useful. Genesis 8:22 declares, "While the earth remaineth, seedtime and harvest, and cold and heat, and summer and winter, and day and night shall not cease." By applying this principal and receiving the word of God in to our lives, we are promised to receive a bountiful harvest. I invite you to reach out to me or connect with me on Instagram and Facebook.

Always remember God blessed you that you may be a blessing.

Warmly,
Byron L.
Aldridge

ABOUT THE AUTHOR

Byron L. Aldridge, is the Senior Pastor and founder, of Shield of Faith Empowerment Center, located in West Memphis, Arkansas. He is a teacher of the word and his message is of faith. God has allowed him to use faith as the vehicle, to release God's promises in his life. He is a witness of the supernatural power of God, where God has performed numerous healings and miracles in the lives of others. Byron is Kingdom builder with a mission and vision, to empower the believer's walk in faith, family, and finances. Byron and his wife, Patrice, live in Marion, Arkansas. They have two children Euri and Bre'onna.

Made in the USA
Coppell, TX
13 February 2021